CW01676614

Contents

Scope and sequence

	Vocabulary	Grammar	Global Citizenship	Project	My sounds
Welcome to Rise and Shine Towers	**Numbers 1–10; colours:** black, blue, brown, orange, pink, purple, red, white, yellow **Classroom objects:** bag, book, chair, desk, door, pencil **Classroom language:** be quiet, listen, look, sit down	Hi! / Hello! What's your name? I'm... / My name's... It's a (desk). It's (brown).	**Let's be friends!**	**A plant pot**	**p, b**
1 Old toys, new toys	**Toys:** ball, car, doll, elephant, robot, tablet, teddy bear, train **Adjectives:** big, small, new, old	What's this? It's a (car). It's an (elephant). It's (small).	**Sharing toys:** new and old toys: bike, kite, music box, plane.	**A class toy swap**	**t, d**
2 All kinds of families **Review 1** Important to me	**Family:** mum, dad, sister, brother, granny, grandad, auntie, uncle **Pets:** bird, cat, dog, fish	Who's this? This is my (dad). I've got a (fish), two (brothers) and (a cat).	**Celebrating families:** cousin, friend, neighbour, pet.	**A family circle**	**g, c**
3 Amazing bodies	**Body parts:** arms, ears, eyes, feet, hands, legs, mouth, nose **Actions:** dance, hop, jump, run	I've got (six ears). I can (jump). I can't (hop).	**Playing games together:** clap, close, move, touch.	**A talent show**	**m, n**
4 Let's eat up **Review 2** All about me	**Food 1:** bananas, bread, cheese, chicken, milk, olives, strawberries, tomatoes **Food 2:** ice cream, milkshake, pizza, sandwiches	I like (bread). I don't like (milk). Do you like (bananas) and (milk)? Yes, I do. / No, I don't.	**Trying different food:** pasta, rice, salad, soup.	**A class lunch**	**h, ch**
5 Nature around us	**Animals:** duck, fox, frog, lizard, mouse, owl, rabbit, turtle **Mini-beasts:** ant, bee, butterfly, ladybird	What can you see? I can see (a fox). Is it (an ant)? Yes, it is. / No, it isn't.	**Exploring nature:** flower, grass, pond, tree.	**A park collage**	**s, f**
6 Let's dress up **Review 3** Around me	**Clothes:** dress, jumper, pyjamas, shirt, shoes, shorts, T-shirt, trousers **Feelings:** cold, happy, hot, sad	I'm wearing (a dress). I'm (happy).	**Appreciating special clothes:** boots, hat, jeans, skirt.	**A special costume doll**	**sh, j**
Goodbye	**Happy holidays! Have a good time!**				
Seasons	**Autumn:** apple, chestnut, fire, leaf, pumpkin, tree; It's windy! **Winter:** boots, gloves, hat, light, scarf, snow; It's snowy! **Spring:** blossom, chick, egg, flower, lamb, rabbit; It's cloudy! **Summer:** beach, picnic, sun hat, sunglasses, sunny, swimming costume; It's sunny!				

My Progress Chart

	Welcome	Unit 1	Unit 2	Unit 3	Unit 4	Unit 5	Unit 6
Listening	I can recognise my words.	I can understand questions.		I can hear my words in dialogues.		I can listen to descriptions and information.	
Reading	I can recognise my letters.	I can make letter sounds.		I can recognise words.		I can match words to pictures.	
Speaking	I can say my words and phrases.	I can answer questions about me and my world.		I can talk about my likes and abilities.		I can describe people and things.	
Writing	I can draw shapes.	I can draw matching lines.		I can circle correct answers.		I can write numbers.	

Welcome to Rise and Shine Towers

Lesson 1

What can you see?

1 Listen and explore. 0.04

2 Point and say.

3 Draw your face.

Lesson 2

1 0.05 Listen and say the colour.

2 0.06 Sing and act. Song

One. It's blue.

I can shine!

3 Colour. Then say.

6 7 8 9 10

1 2 3 4 5

Lesson 3

1 0.08 Listen, point and say.

2 0.09 Listen or watch.

I can shine!

3 Draw, colour and say.

1

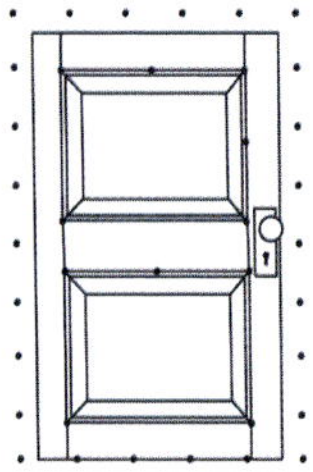

2

 Story language *It's my (door). It's (blue).*

Lessons 4 and 5

1 0.10 Listen and find.

2 0.11 Listen and say.

3 0.12 Listen and say.

I can shine!

4 Play school!

Global Citizen
Let's be friends

Lessons 6 and 7

1 0.13 Listen and colour.

2 0.14 How old are they? Listen and circle.

1  a 6 b 8

2  a 4 b 6

3  a 4 b 6

4  a 6 b 8

I can shine!

3 Play!

Think and share!

New friends

Step 1 Review

4 Follow and say.

Step 2 Create

5 Colour.

Time to shine!

6 Show and say.

1 Old toys, new toys

Lesson 1

What can you see?

1 (1.01) Listen and explore.

2 (1.02) Listen, point and say.

3 Stick and say.

4 Watch and listen.

Lesson 2

1 1.03 Sing and act. Song

2 1.05 Listen and circle.

What's this?
It's a car.

I can shine!

3 Ask and answer about toys.

Lesson 3

1 Which toys can you see in the story? Point and say *yes* or *no*.

2 1.07 Listen or watch.

Rise and Shine

Towers

 Story value A story about caring for and recycling toys

Let's imagine!

I can shine!

3 Circle Dexter's favourite toy.

4 Act out.

Lesson 4

1 1.08 Listen and find. **2** 1.09 Listen, point and say.

3 1.10 Listen and say.

It's new.
It's blue.
It's old.
It's small.

4 Find and colour. Then say.

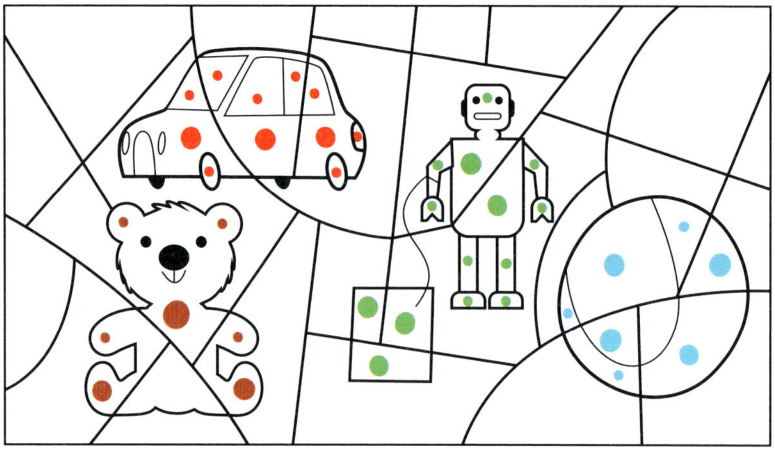

Lesson 5

1 1.11 Listen and point.

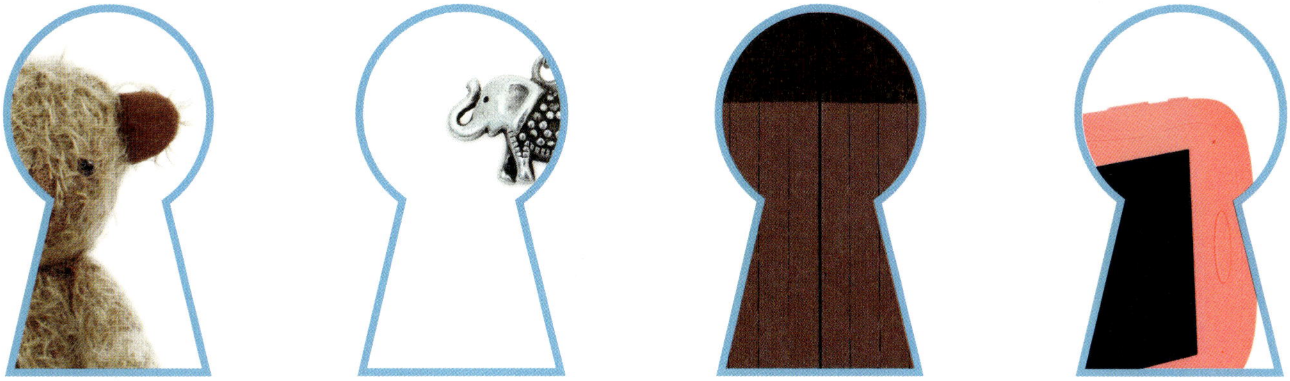

2 Look and play.

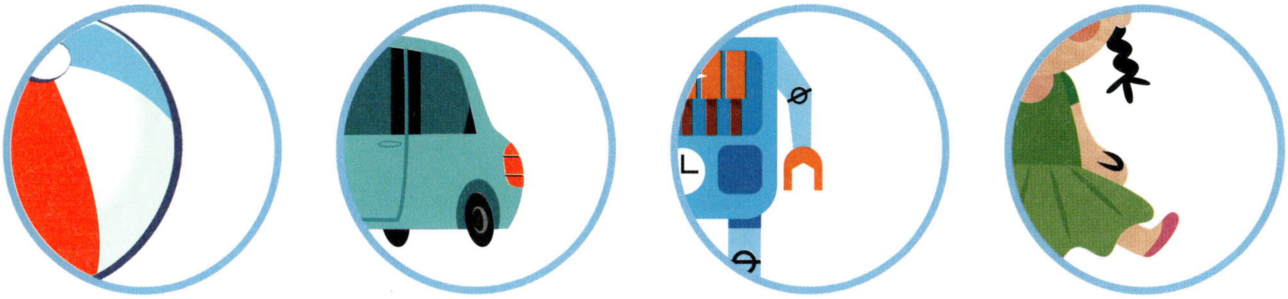

3 1.12 Listen and say.

My sounds

t

d

I can shine!

4 Cut out and guess the toys.

Lesson 6

1 1.15 Listen, look and find. **2** 1.16 Listen, point and say.

3 Circle old toys in blue. Circle new toys in green.

4 Watch and listen.

Lesson 7

Playing with friends

1 Look and match. Find.

2 1.17 Listen and circle.

1

2

I can shine!

3 Choose a toy. Let's play!

Let's have a class toy swap!

Step 1 Review

1 1.17a Listen and circle.

2 Choose a toy. Draw and colour.

3 Describe the toy.

4 Think! Choose a toy for the box. Circle.

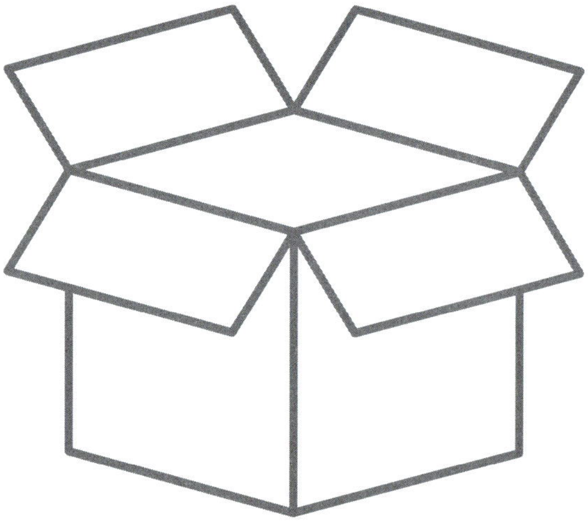

Step 2 Create

5 Draw your toy for the class toy swap.

6 Add your toy to a class toy swap poster.

7 Describe your toy.

8 Talk with your friend. Guess your friend's toy.

Time to shine!

9 Share your toy with the class.

2 All kinds of families

Lesson 1

What can you see?

1 2.01 Listen and explore.

2 2.02 Listen, point and say.

3 Stick and say. **4** Watch and listen.

Lesson 2

1 2.03 Sing and act. Song

2 2.05 Listen and circle.

1
2
3
4

Who's this?
This is my dad.

I can shine!

3 Ask and answer for Dexter.

I can ask about family.

Lesson 3

1 Who's in the story? Point and say *yes* or *no*.

2 2.07 Listen or watch.

 Story value A story about appreciating family and friends

I can shine!

3 Circle Elena's family.

4 Act out.

I can understand a story about different families.

Lesson 4

1 2.08 Listen and find.

2 2.09 Listen, point and say.

3 2.10 Listen and say.

I've got a fish.

4 Follow and find. Say.

Lesson 5

1 2.11 Listen, point and say.

1

2

2 Look and play.

3 2.12 Listen and say.

My sounds

I can shine!

4 Cut out and say.

I can describe my family and pets.

Lesson 6

1 2.15 Listen, point and say. **2** 2.16 Listen and find.

a

b

c

d

3 Who do you do these things with? Look, think and match.

1

2

3

4 Watch and listen.

Lesson 7

Thanking people

1 Who's the card for? Look, point and say.

2.17 Then listen and check.

2 Who's the card for? Join the dots and say.

I can shine!

3 Let's thank someone!

I can thank people.

Let's make a family circle!

Step 1 Review

1 Look, point and say.

2 Who's in your family? Tell a friend.

3 Think! Who is important to you? Say.

Step 2 Create

4 Who are your special people? Draw.

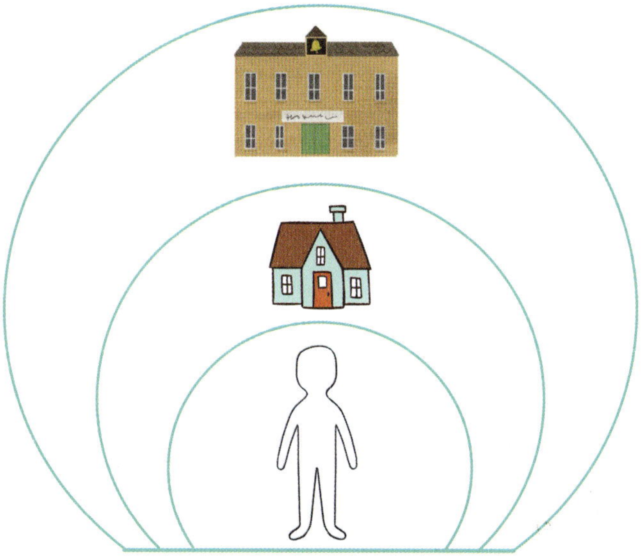

5 Make your family circle.

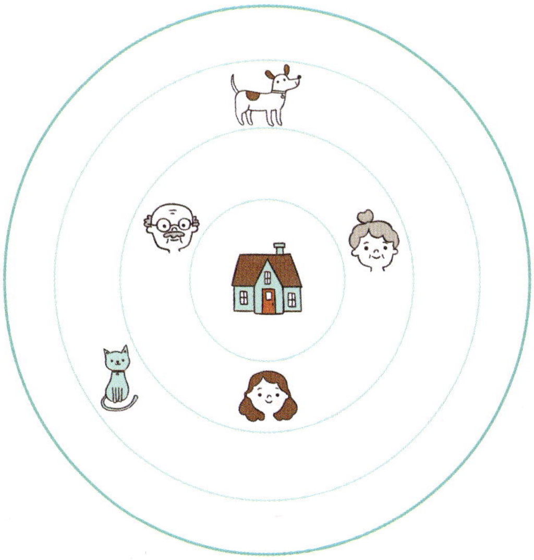

Time to shine!

6 Show your family circle to the class.

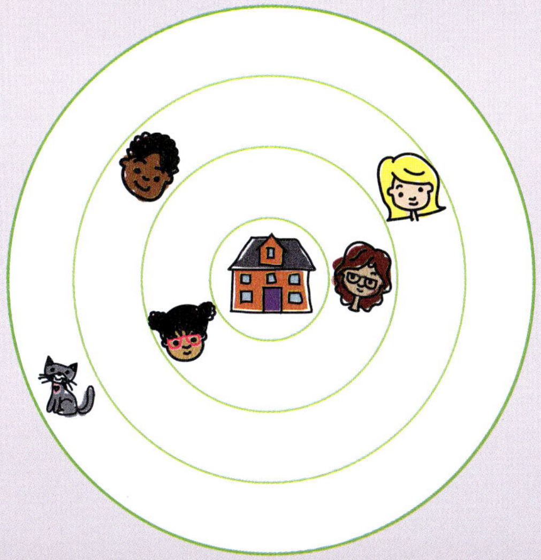

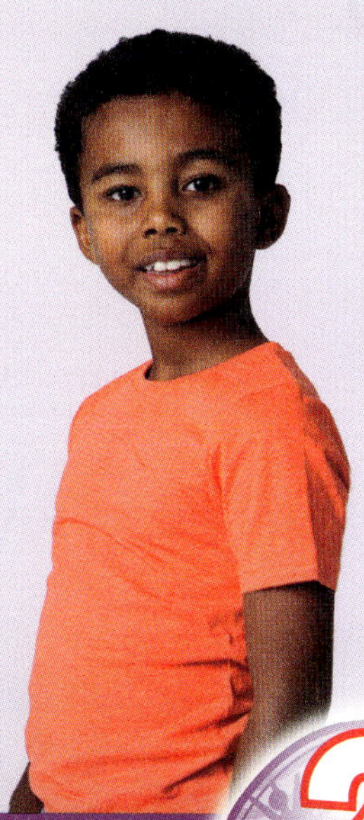

I can appreciate all kinds of families!

Review 1 Important to me

1 2.18 Listen and find the toys.

2 2.18a Whose toys? Listen, point and say.

3 Look and point. Then ask and answer about toys.

Mini-project

4 Draw a wrapped present. Tell a friend.

Think about my progress

5 How many words do you know? Which story and song is your favourite? Tell a friend.

Time to shine!

6 Look and tick (✓).

3 Amazing bodies

Lesson 1

What can you see?

1 3.01 Listen and explore.

2 3.02 Listen, point and say.

3 Stick and say. **4** Watch and listen.

Lesson 2

1 3.03 Sing and act. Song

2 3.05 Listen and circle.

I've got three eyes.

I can shine!

3 Play a guessing game.

I can talk about my body.

Lesson 3

1 Who's in the story? Point and say *yes* and *no*.

2 3.07 Listen or watch.

I can shine!

3 Who can dance? Tick (✓) and say.

4 Act out.

I can understand a story about different abilities.

Lesson 4

1 3.08 Listen and find. **2** 3.09 Listen, point and say.

3 3.10 Listen and say.

4 Follow, find and draw. Then say.

Lesson 5

1 3.11 Listen and point.

a

b

c

d

2 Look and play.

3 3.12 Listen and say.

My sounds

I can shine!

4 Cut out and play!

I can describe my abilities.

Lesson 6

1 3.15 Listen, point and say. **2** 3.16 Listen and find.

3 Look and circle. Then say.

4 Watch and listen.

Playing together

Lesson 7

1 Look, match and say.

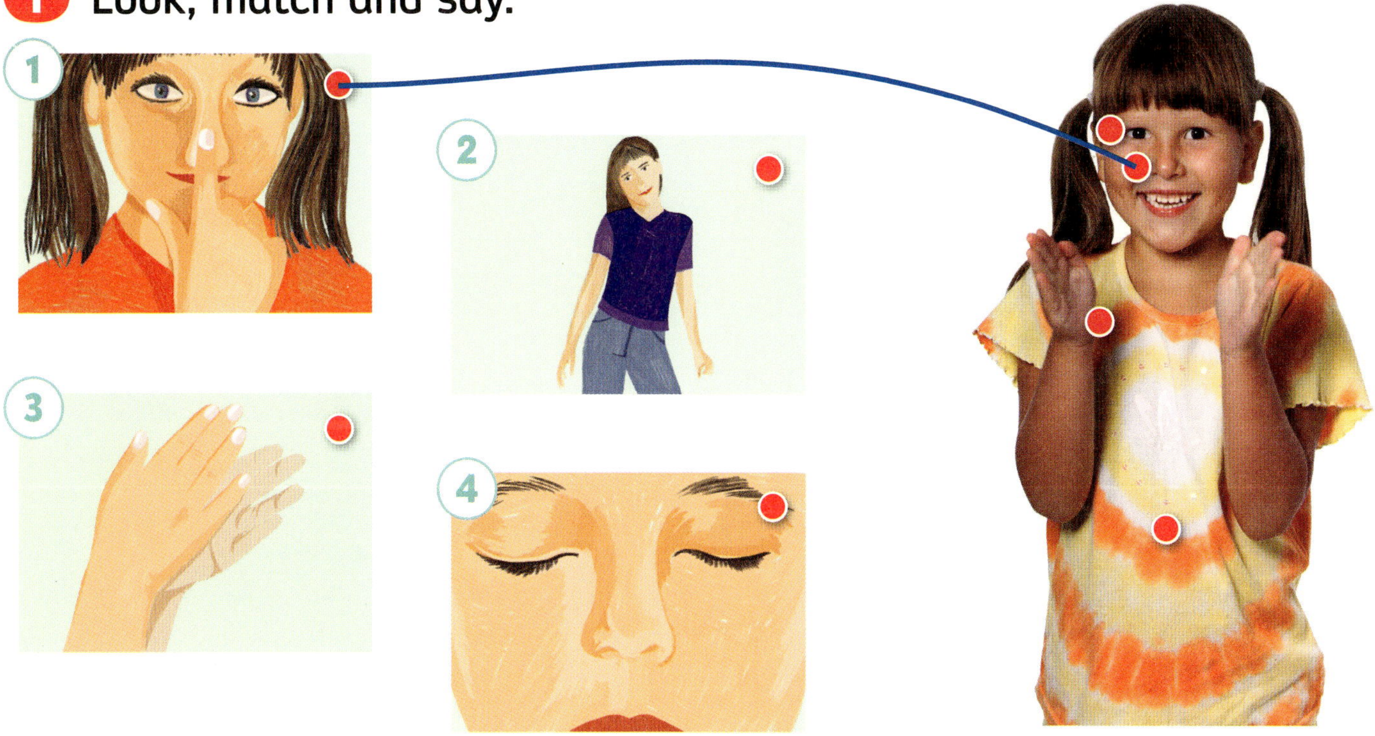

2 3.17 Listen and circle.

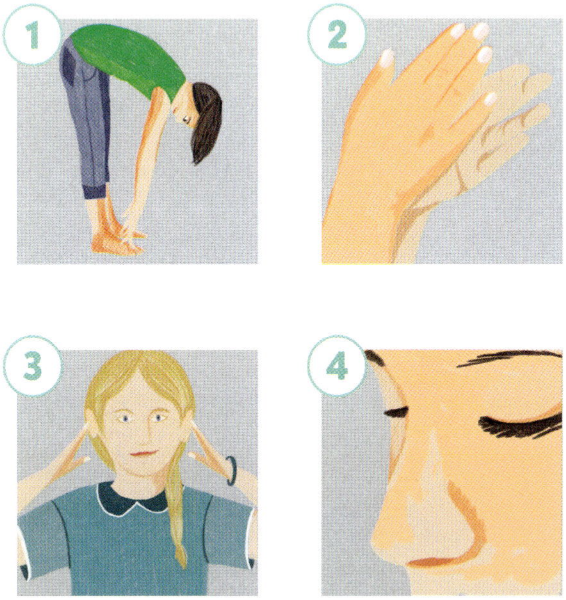

I can shine!

3 Let's play a game!

I can give instructions.

Let's have a class talent show!

Step 1 Review

1 Look, point and say.

2 What can you do? Draw ☺ or ☹ and say.

3 Think! Circle and challenge a friend.

Step 2 Create

4 How many have you got? Match.

1

2

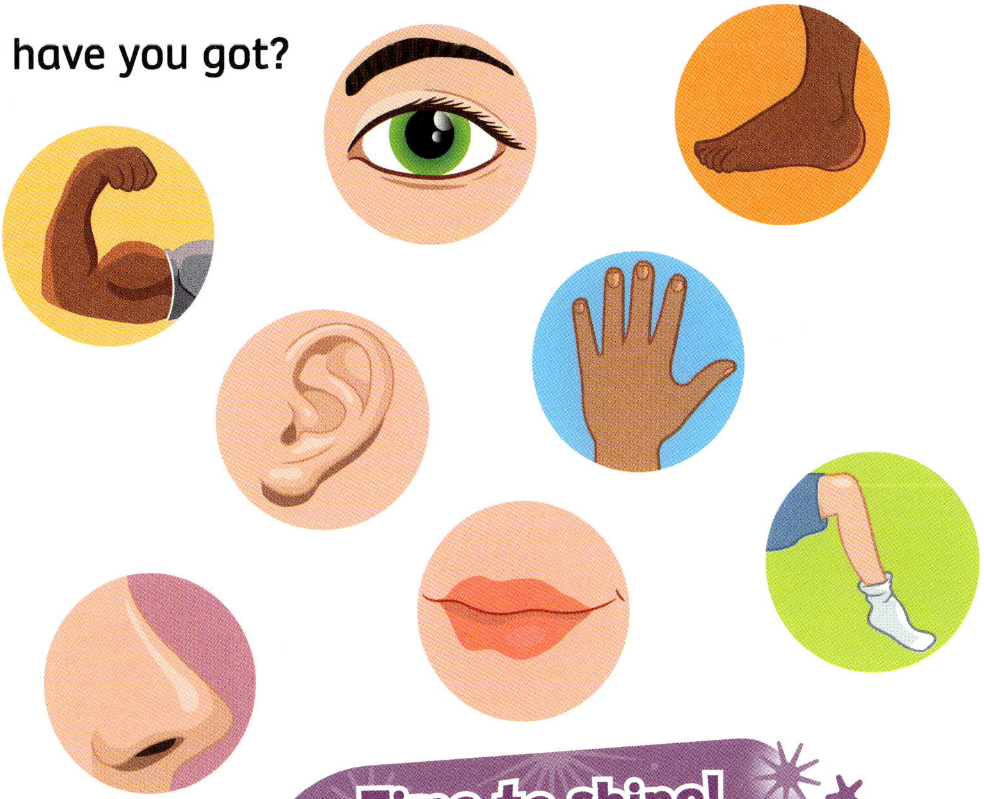

5 Make a body poster.

Time to shine!

6 Show your class what you can do!

I can show what I can do!

4 Let's eat up

Lesson 1

What can you see?

1 4.01 Listen and explore.

2 4.02 Listen, point and say.

3 Stick and say. 4 Watch and listen.

Lesson 2

1 4.03 Sing and act. Song

2 4.05 Listen and draw ☺ or ☹.

I like chicken.
I don't like bananas.

I can shine!

3 And you? Choose and say.

I can say what food I like.

Lesson 3

1 What food can you see in the story? Tick (✓).

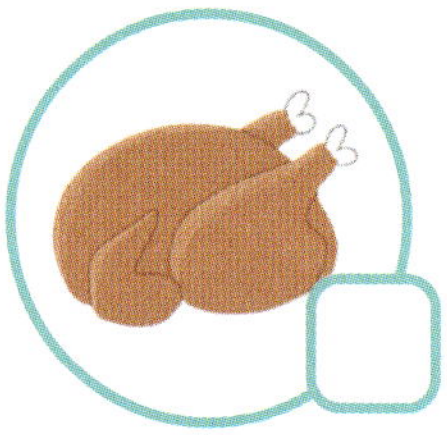

2 4.07 Listen or watch.

Rise and Shine — Towers

 Story value A story about likes and dislikes

Let's imagine!

I can shine!

3 Tick (✓) or cross (✗) for Bruno.

4 Act out.

I can understand a story about likes and dislikes.

Lesson 4

1 4.08 Listen and find.

2 4.09 Listen, point and say. Then trace.

3 4.10 Listen and say.

Do you like bread?
Yes, I do. / No, I don't.

Chant

Do you like pizza? – No, I don't.
Do you like milkshake? – Yes, I do.
Do you like milkshake?
Pink, pink, milkshake?
Yes, I do, yes, I do, yes, I do!

4 4.10a Listen and tick (✓) or cross (✗). Answer for you. Then ask a friend.

Lesson 5

1 4.11 Listen and draw ☺ or ☹.

2 Look and play.

3 4.12 Listen and say.

My sounds

Happy **ch**ickens **h**op and **ch**ant.

I can shine!

4 Cut out and sort: ☺ or ☹. Ask and answer.

I can ask and answer about food.

Global Citizen

I like different foods

Lesson 6

1 4.15 Listen, point and say.

2 4.16 Listen and find. Then trace.

3 Circle the odd one out.

4 Watch and listen.

Lesson 7

It's lunchtime!

1 Look, match and say.

2 4.17 Listen and tick (✓).

1

2

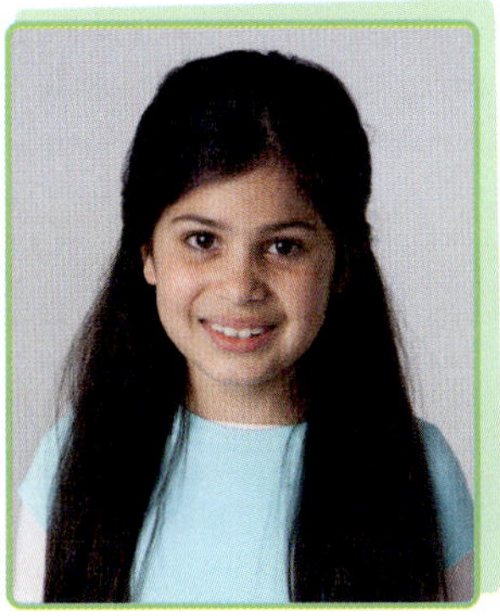

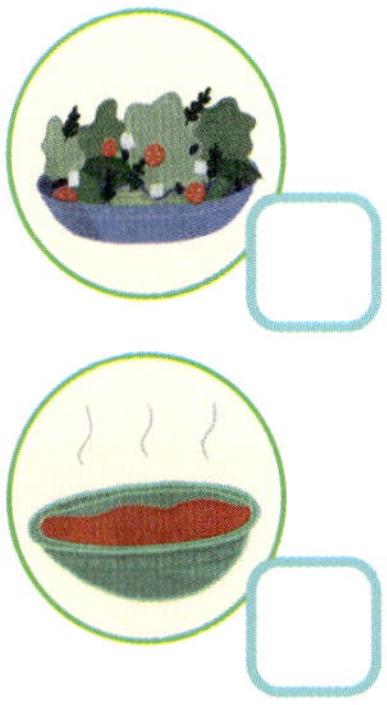

3 And you? Circle the food you like.

I can shine!

4 Let's order some food!

I can ask for food from a menu.

Let's make a class lunch!

Step 1 Review

1 Trace and match.

2 Circle the food you like.

bread
strawberries
cheese
tomatoes

milk
chicken
olives
bananas

3 Ask and answer.

4 Think! Tick (✓) your favourite lunch. Ask your friend.

Step 2 Create

5 Think about your favourite food. Draw.

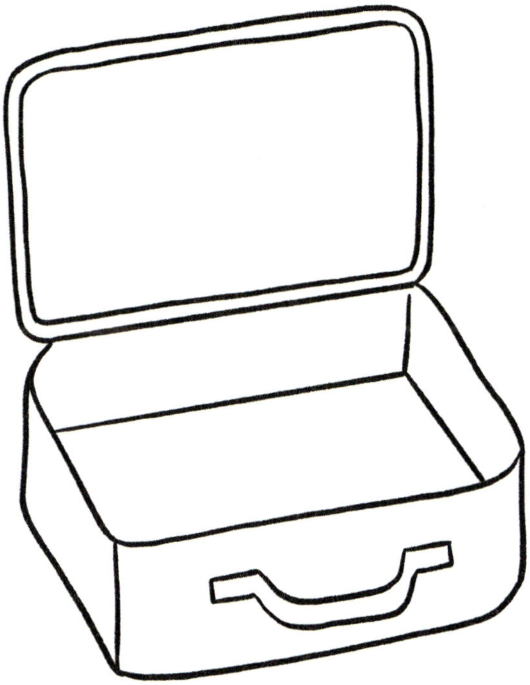

6 Make or draw your lunch plate.

7 Ask a friend.

Time to shine!

8 Share your lunch plate with the class.

I can share lunch with my class!

Review 2 All about me

1 4.18 Listen and find the food.

2 Look and point. Then ask and answer.

3 What can you do? Point and say. Then match.

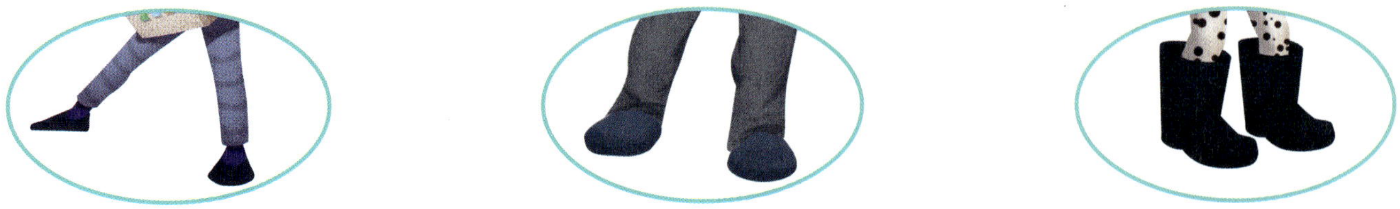

Mini-project

4 Draw or make an *All about me* card.

Think about my progress

5 How many words do you know? Which story and song is your favourite? Tell a friend.

Time to shine!

6 What can you do now? Look and tick (✓).

5 Nature around us

Lesson 1

What can you see?

1 5.01 Listen and explore.

Tell me!
What animals are in your park?

2 5.02 Listen, point and say.

3 Stick and say.

4 Watch and listen.

Lesson 2

1 5.03 Sing and act. **Song**

2 5.05 Listen and circle.

What can you see?
I can see a frog.

I can shine!

3 Count all the animals. Say.

I can name animals.

Lesson 3

1 Which animals are in the story? Tick (✓).

2 5.07 Listen or watch.

Let's imagine!
What can Bruno see?
Guess and draw.

I can shine!

3 Which animal are the children following? Circle.

4 Act out.

I can understand a story about animals.

Lesson 4

1 5.08 Listen and find.

2 5.09 Listen, point and say. Then trace.

3 5.10 Listen and say.

Is it a ladybird?
Yes, it is. / No, it isn't.

Chant

Look at the flower. What can you see?
Is it a ladybird? No, it isn't.
Is it a bee? Yes, it is!

4 Draw, trace and circle. Ask a friend.

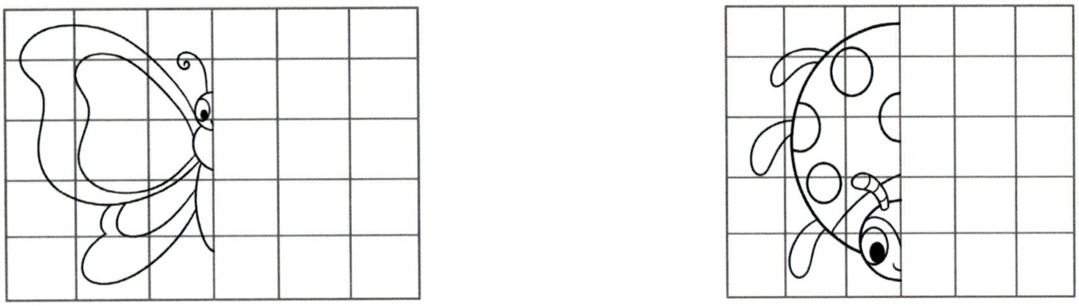

1 bee / butterfly

2 ladybird / ant

Lesson 5

1 5.11 Listen and tick (✓).

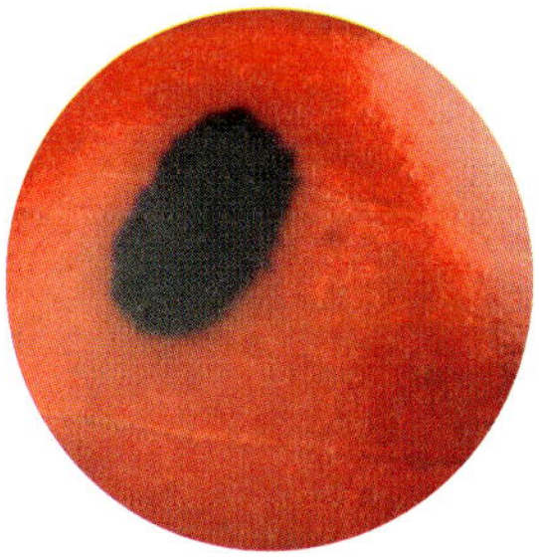

1 butterfly ☐
owl ☐

2 ant ☐
bee ☐

3 ladybird ☐
ant ☐

2 Look and play.

What can you see? Is it a butterfly?

No, it isn't. I can see an owl.

3 5.12 Listen and say.

My sounds

Seven smiling frogs sitting by a flower!

I can shine!

4 Cut out and guess the animals.

I can ask and answer about animals.

Lesson 6

1 5.15 Listen, point and say.

2 5.16 Listen and find. Then trace.

3 Look and match. Then circle the animals that live near you.

4 Watch and listen.

Lesson 7

In the park

1 Read, look and number.

owl ☐ duck ☐ mouse ☐ butterfly ☐

Let's find a butterfly!

2 5.17 Listen and match.

pond

tree

flowers

I can shine!

3 Let's explore the park!

I can find animals in the park.

Let's make a park collage!

Step 1 Review

1 Find and trace.

1 duck 2 turtle 3 fox 4 mouse

5 rabbit 6 owl 7 lizard 8 frog

2 Colour two animals.

3 Guess your friend's animals.

4 Think! Tick (✓) homes for your animals.

Step 2 Create

5 Think about the homes. Draw an animal for each home.

6 Make your park collage.

7 Share with a friend.

Time to shine!

8 Show your park collage to the class.

I can explore nature!

5

6 Let's dress up

Lesson 1

What can you see?

1 6.01 Listen and explore.

Tell me!
What colour are your clothes?

2 6.02 Listen, point and say.

3 Stick and say. **4** Watch and listen.

Lesson 2

1 6.03 Sing and act. **Song**

2 6.05 Listen and tick (✓).

I'm wearing a shirt.

I can shine!

3 What are you wearing today? Say.

I'm wearing a blue T-shirt. I'm wearing brown trousers.

I can talk about my clothes.

Lesson 3

1 Which clothes can you see in the story? Tick (✓).

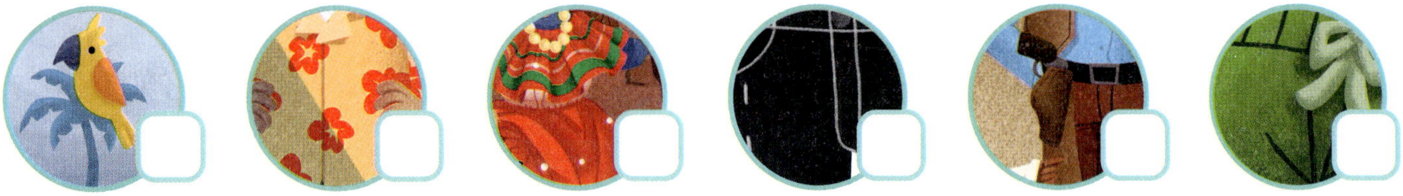

2 6.07 Listen or watch.

Let's imagine!

Design a T-shirt for Mia.

I can shine!

3 What is Elena wearing? Tick (✓).

- a shirt and shorts ☐
- a dress ☐
- pyjamas ☐

4 Act out.

I can understand a story about clothes.

1 6.08 Listen and find. **2** 6.09 Listen and match. Say.

happy sad hot cold

3 6.10 Listen and say.

I'm happy.

Chant

I'm wearing a jumper. I'm hot.
I'm wearing pyjamas. I'm cold.
I'm wearing a shirt. I'm happy.
I'm wearing a dress. Oh no! I'm sad!

4 Follow and write. Act out with a friend.

1 I'm ________.

2 I'm ________.

3 I'm ________.

4 I'm ________.

Lesson 5

1 6.11 Listen and match. Circle and say.

1 
2 
3 
4 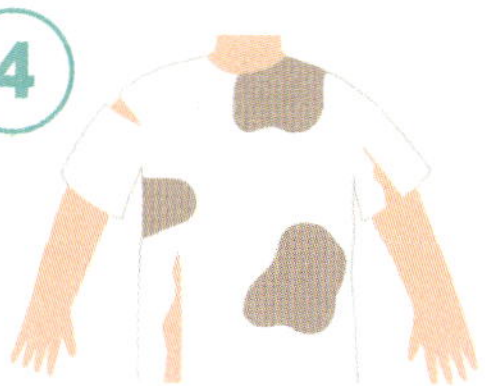

a 
hot / cold

b 
happy / sad

c 
hot / cold

d 
happy / sad

2 Look and play.

I'm wearing shorts. Brr!

Cold!

3 6.12 Listen and say.

My sounds

sh **j**

One, two – shiny shoes.
One, two, three – jumper and jeans!

I can shine!

4 Cut out and play!

I'm wearing pyjamas. I'm cold!

I can describe my clothes and feelings.

Lesson 6

1 6.15 Listen, look and find. **2** 6.16 Listen and point. Say.

boots hat jeans skirt

3 Match and say.

Think and share!

Have you got special clothes?
When do you wear them?

4 Watch and listen.

Lesson 7

At a party

1 Read and number.

2 6.17 Listen and check.

Come to my dress-up party!

Wear ...

☐ ... a dress!

☐ ... a hat!

☐ ... pyjamas!

☐ ... big ears!

Saturday, in the park!

3 And you? Circle and write.

a shirt a hat shoes jeans

Come to a dress-up party!

Wear a special jumper / dress.

Wear a skirt / T-shirt, big boots / ears, and

____________________!

I can shine!

4 Let's dress up for a party!

I can invite friends to a party.

Let's make a special costume!

Step 1 Review

1 Find and write.

dress jumper pyjamas shirt shoes shorts trousers T-shirt

s ___ ___ ___ ___ ☐

T-___ ___ ___ ___ ___ ☐

j ___ ___ ___ ___ ___ ☐

s ___ ___ ___ ___ ___ ☐

s ___ ___ ___ ___ ☐

p ___ ___ ___ ___ ___ ___ ☐

d ___ ___ ___ ___ ☐

t ___ ___ ___ ___ ___ ___ ___ ☐

2 Tick (✓) the clothes you are wearing. Then write.

I'm wearing ________________ and ________________.

3 Circle how you feel. Tell a friend.

4 Think! What are your favourite clothes? Write.

I like my ________________.

Step 2 Create

5 Think about a special party costume. Draw and write.

My special costume.

I'm wearing ________

and ________.

6 Make a special costume doll.

7 Invite a friend to your party!

Come to my party! Wear a big hat!

Time to shine!

8 Share your special costume dolls.

Look at me! I'm wearing a hat. I'm happy.

I can appreciate special clothes!

Review 3 Around me

1 6.18 Listen and find the clothes.

2 Look and point. Then say.

I can see a bee.
Look at the tree.

3 Read and write.

jumper   jeans   T-shirt   hat   shorts   skirt   dress

I'm wearing…

1 ____________ 2 ____________ 3 ____________ 4 ____________

Mini-project

4 Design. Then write and say.

Look! I'm wearing a ______________.
I'm happy!

Time to shine!

6 Read and tick (✓).

1 I can read animals and clothes words. ☐

2 I can talk about animals and clothes. ☐

3 I can find animals in nature. ☐

4 I can choose clothes and dress up. ☐

Think about my progress

5 Read and complete.

I know ☐ nature words.

I know ☐ clothes words.

My favourite story is in Unit ☐.

My favourite song is in Unit ☐.

Goodbye from Rise and Shine Towers

What can you see?

1 7.01 Listen and explore.

2 7.02 Listen again and tick (✓).

books desks bike chairs tablet pizza

3 Watch.

Goodbye! Goodbye!
From Rise and Shine Towers
Happy holidays!
Have a good time!

Goodbye Elena, Bruno, too
Dexter, Mia, see you soon.
Goodbye Granny,
have a good time!
Goodbye, Goodbye,
Rise and Shine Towers.

4 7.03 Sing and act. **Song**

I can shine!

5 Draw your face and colour. Then say.

Level 1

It's autumn!

1 8.01 Listen, point and say.

2 8.02 Sing and act. Listen again and circle. Song

3 Make an autumn tree.

Winter holidays

1 8.05 Listen, point and say.

2 8.06 Sing and act. Listen again and point. Song

3 Make a snowman.

Spring is here!

1 8.09 Listen, point and say.

2 8.10 Listen and sing. Stand up when you hear these things.

Song

3 Make an egg surprise.

Sunny summer days

1 8.13 Listen, point and say.

2 8.14 Sing and act. Listen again and number. Song

3 Make a beach in a jar.

Pearson Education Limited
KAO Two
KAO Park
Hockham Way
Harlow, Essex
CM17 9SR
England
and Associated Companies throughout the world.

pearsonenglish.com

First published 2021
Fifth impression 2024

ISBN: 978-1-292-36996-9

Set in Daytona Pro Primary

Printed in Slovakia by Neografia

Acknowledgements
Seasons lessons written by Mary Roulston

The publisher would like to thank the following for their kind permission to reproduce their photographs:

123RF.com: Krystian Krawczyk 15, Marilyn Barbone 60, Oliver Moh 60; **Getty Images:** AbimelecOlan 70, Anthony Harvie 19, Daniel Grill 79, Esther Moreno Martinez/EyeEm 17, iStock/Getty Images Plus 14, 14, 15, Jose Luis Pelaez Inc 26, Kevin van der Leek Photography 16, Kinzie+Riehm 9, Maskot 26, Pascal Broze 16, Paul-Gino Guevarra/EyeEm 16, Piyamas Chaiyaprap/EyeEm 16, REB Images 80, RichVintage 70, SDI Productions 27, Tetra Images - PT Images 78, THEPALMER 16, Tzille Blanquel/EyeEm 70, ViewStock 16, Westend61 17, Yogesh Mohite/EyeEm 81; **Pearson Education Ltd:** Jon Barlow 15, 25, 27, 29, 37, 39, 41, 47, 49, 51, 59, 61, 63, 69, 71, 73, 78, 79, 80, 81; **Shutterstock.com:** 69, Akif Oztoprak 17, aldegonde 14, Alesikka 61, Alex Staroseltsev 59, Algonga 61, Anatoliy Lukich 26, Anna Jurkovska 60, archideaphoto 39, Arisa_J 71, benedektibor 15, canbedone 17, Christos Georghiou 36, 36, 41, 41, DianaFinch 61, Flas100 49, Gorgev 26, ILYA AKINSHIN 17, jadimages 59, Lucky Creative 61, MatoomMi 69, Ociacia 14, Olga Sapegina 39, Patty Chan 49, Prostock-studio 27, StevenRussellSmithPhotos 61, studiovin 17, sweetheart studio 15, Tr1sha 17, VikiVector 79, Vitalii Hulai 59

Cover Image: Front: **Alamy Stock Photo:** Visuals Stock Cover with course characters (illustrated by BluBlu Studios)

All other images © Pearson Education

Illustrated by BluBlu Studios (course characters); Becky Down/The Bright Agency: pp.14, 37 (activity 1), 43, 44, 45, 50 (activity 4), 62 (activity 4), 63 (activity 5), 68, 69, 72 (emojis); Camila Galindo/ Beehive illustration: pp.24, 55, 56, 58, 62 (activity 1); Denise Holmes/The Bright Agency: pp.19, 27, 29 (top family circle); Julie Ingham /The Bright Agency: pp. 38, 60, 61; Edyta Karaban/Sylvie Poggio: p.25 (family portraits); Anna Kazimi/Beehive Illustration: pp.78–81; Maria Kiryakova pp.18 (the doll in the shelf), 25 (the top left family), 40 (the girl with pink ears, the ballerina), 69 (activity 1 items 1 and c), 80 (activity 1), 81 (activity 1); Adam Linley/Beehive Illustration: pp.3, 5, 17, 18 (line drawings), 28, 29 (bottom family circle), 40, 72 (activity 1), 75 (activity 4), all I can Shine! sticker artworks throughout; Steph Marshall/The Bright Agency: pp.26, 48, 49, 70, 71; Xavier Mula/Beehive Illustration: p.16, all global citizenship banners: pp.8, 16, 26, 38, 48, 60, 70; Lynne Moulding / Independent: pp.82–93; Alex Naidoo/Sylvie Poggio: pp. 9, 18 (shelves), 33, 46, 47 (activity 1), 50 (activity 1), 74, 76; David Ortu / Beehive Illustration: p.65; Hyphen SA (Zacharias Papadopoulos); Mark Ruffl e/Beehive Illustration: pp.7, 11, 75 (activity 6), 77, My sounds p:15, 25, 31, 37, 47, 59.

https://www.un.org/sustainabledevelopment/
The content of this publication has not been approved by the United Nations and does not reflect the views of the United Nations or its officials or Member States.

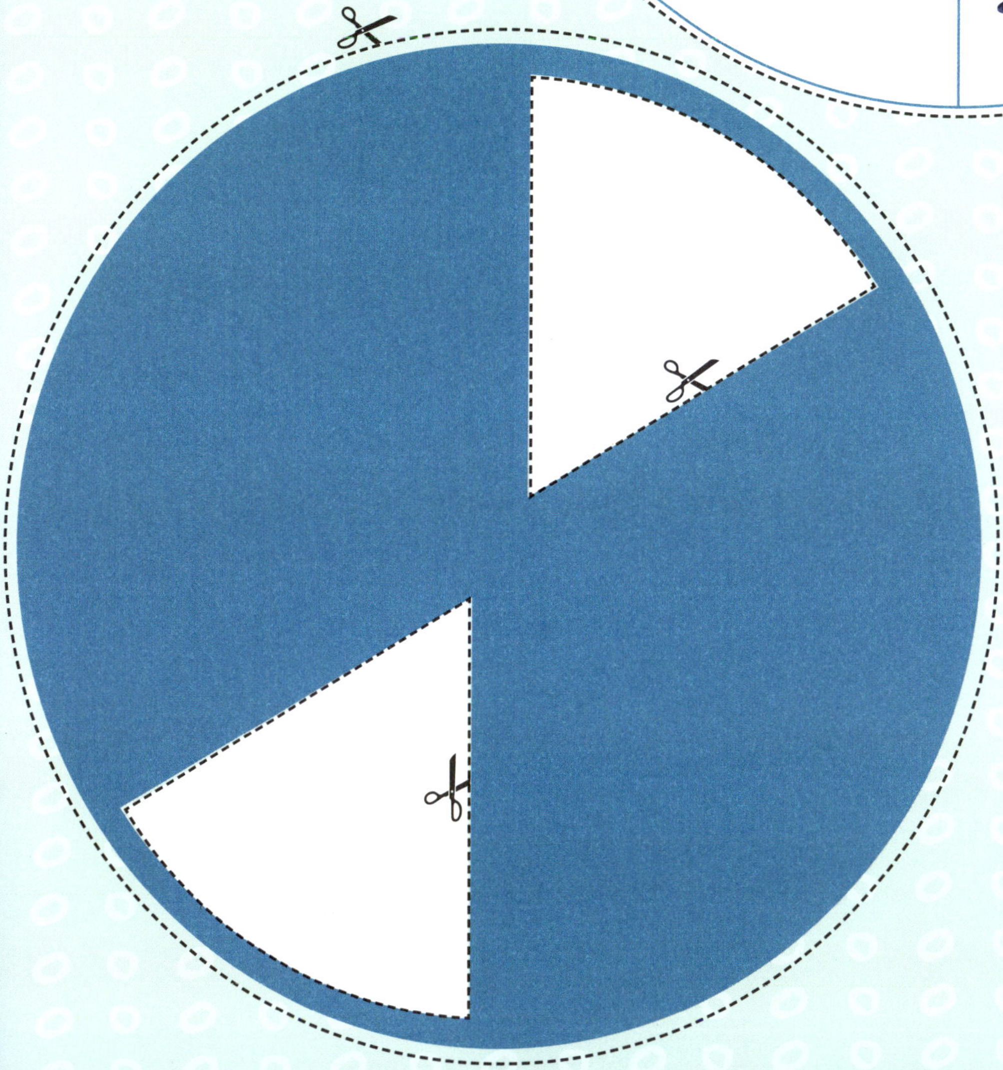

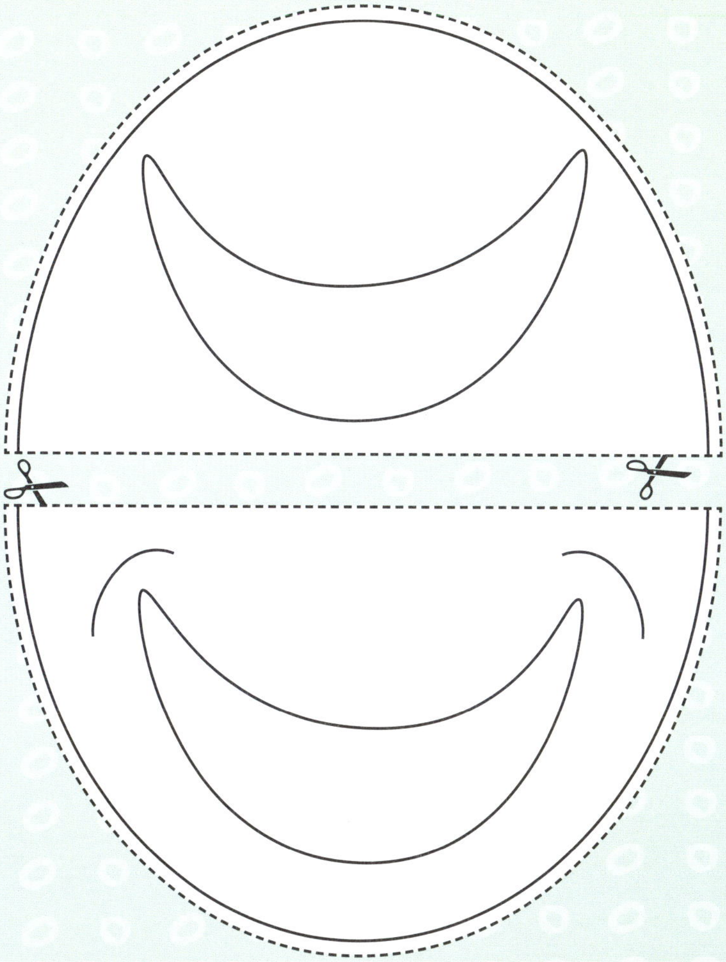

——— fold

------- cut

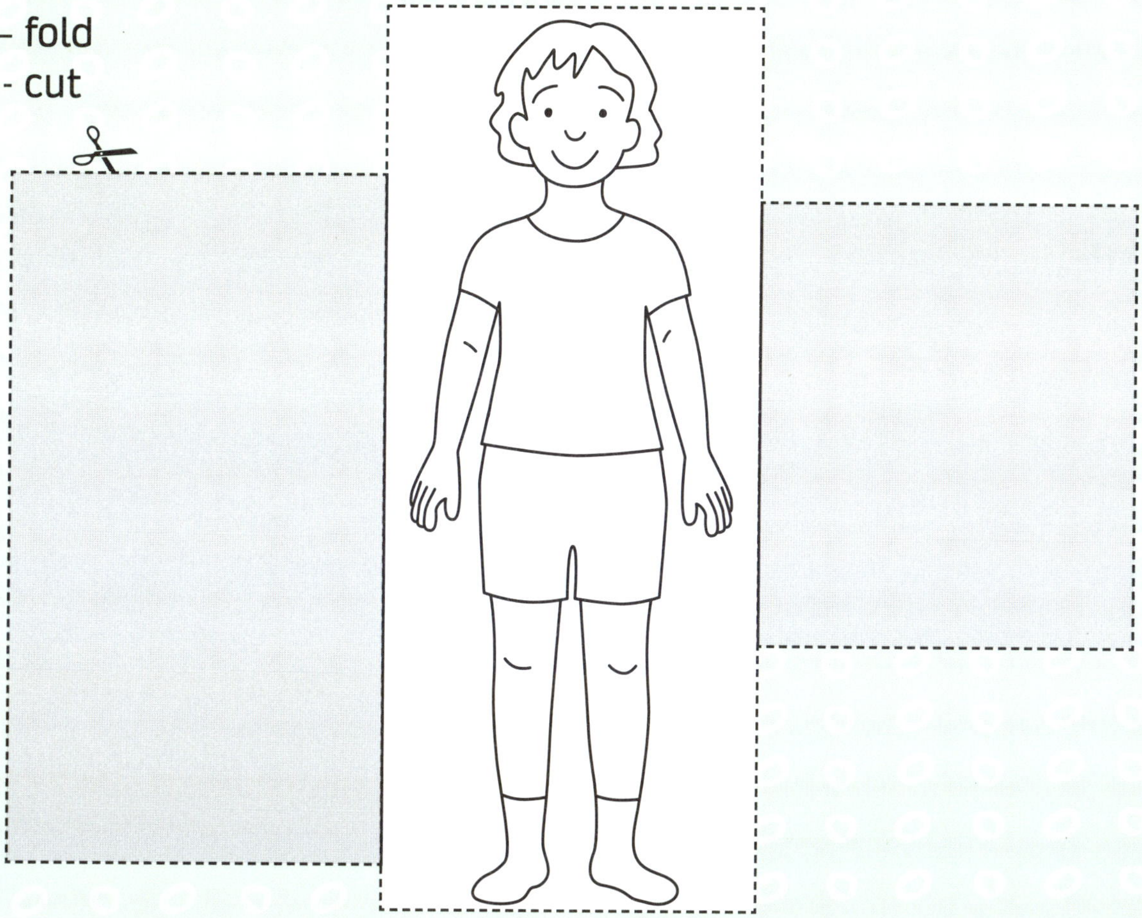

Rise and Shine stickers

Unit 1

pages 10–11

Unit 2

pages 20–21

Unit 3

pages 32–33

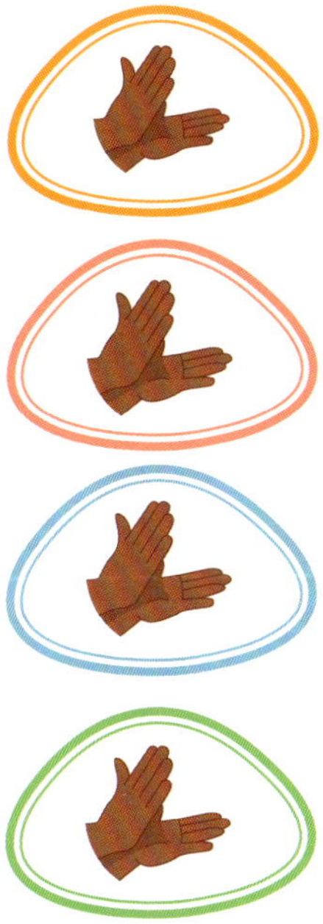

Unit 4

pages 42–43

Unit 5

pages 54-55

Unit 6

pages 64-65